Everyday Heroes

I Talk You Talk Press

CONTENTS

I Talk You Talk Press

1. THE PIZZA GUY

Oliver works for a pizza company. He delivers pizzas. He rides a small motorbike. The motorbike has a big box on the back. Oliver puts the pizzas in the box, and takes them to customers' houses. He likes his job, but he doesn't like it when it rains.

Today, it is raining. Many people don't want to go out, so they order pizzas. Oliver is very busy. Now, he is at the pizza shop.

"Here are the pizzas for your next delivery," says Eddie. "Two for an apartment on West Street, and one for an apartment on Seaside Road."

"I'll go to West Street first," says Oliver. "It is not so far."

He takes the pizzas outside, and puts them in the box on the back of his bike. It is 7:30pm, and it is dark and cold. He puts his helmet on and rides out of the pizza shop car park.

Fifteen minutes later, he arrives at the apartment on West Street. He parks his bike in the car park and checks the address on the receipt.

Apartment number five three two, he thinks. *I have never been to that apartment. They are new customers.*

He takes two pizzas out of the box and takes the elevator up to the 5th floor. When the elevator stops, he gets out. The apartment building is old and dark. There are few lights. He finds apartment 532 and rings the doorbell. There is no answer. He rings it again. No one comes. He knocks on the door loudly. Again, no one comes.

Oliver is not happy. *Is this a joke?* he thinks.

Sometimes, people call the pizza company and order a pizza. They give the wrong address. They think it is funny. It is not funny for Oliver.

He knocks on the door again. "Your pizza is here!" he shouts. There is no answer.

I give up, thinks Oliver. *I will take the pizzas back to the shop. It is a joke.* Just then, he smells something strange.

What's that? he thinks. *It smells like gas.*

He puts his face close to the door. The smell of gas is stronger. He opens the letterbox. He cannot see inside, but he can smell gas. It is a strong smell.

This is very dangerous! he thinks.

He shouts through the letterbox, "Hello! Can you hear me? Are you OK?"

There is no answer.

I have to go inside, thinks Oliver. *Maybe the people need help.*

He puts the pizza boxes on the floor, and pushes the door. It is locked. He pushes harder. The door moves a little. Then, he runs and hits the door very hard. The lock breaks, and the door opens. The smell of gas is very strong. The lights are on in the apartment. He goes into the living room and sees a man and a woman and a young girl. They are lying on sofas in front of the fire. They look like they are sleeping. Oliver shouts, "Are you OK?", but the people don't move.

Oliver runs out of the apartment and takes out his phone. He calls for an ambulance and he calls the police.

He says, "There is a family. I think there is a problem with the gas. They are not moving. Maybe they are dead. Please come quickly. The address is five three two Apartment Building One, West Street."

Oliver waits outside the apartment. Ten minutes later, two ambulances and the police come. A worker from the gas company also comes. The ambulance staff run into the apartment. The worker from the gas company turns the gas switch off. The police talk to Oliver and ask him many questions.

The ambulance staff come out of the apartment with the family members. The family members are lying on stretchers, and the ambulance staff are carrying them.

"Are they OK?" asks Oliver. "Are they alive?"

"Yes, they are alive," says a woman. "Thanks to you. You saved their lives. You are a very brave young man."

The ambulance staff carry the family down to the ambulances.

"Well done!" says a policeman.

Oliver smiles. "I didn't do anything special," he says.

Just then, Oliver's phone rings. It is Eddie from the pizza company.

"Oliver, where are you? The customer on Seaside Road called us. She is very angry! She has been waiting a long time for her pizza!"

"Tell her I'm sorry," says Oliver. "I had a small problem at the apartment on West Street, but I will go to her apartment now!"

When Oliver finishes his delivery and goes back to the pizza shop, his boss is waiting for him.

Oh no, thinks Oliver. *Maybe I am in trouble. I took a long time.*

"Oliver," says Vicky, his boss. "The police called us. They told us about the gas problem. You saved the people in the house. You did a very good thing. You are a hero. I'm going to give you some extra money this month. I'm going to give you an extra hundred dollars."

Oliver smiles. "Thank you!" he says. "But really, I didn't do anything special!"

2. THE BIKER GANG

Lydia is excited and nervous. Today is her wedding. Now, she is at home with her father and sister. She is wearing a pretty, white dress.

"You look beautiful," says Katy, her sister.

"Yes," says her father. "You look wonderful. Ben is a lucky man."

Lydia looks in the mirror. Her hair and makeup are perfect. The dress looks wonderful.

Then, they hear a car outside. Her father looks out of the window.

"The wedding car is here," he says. "Come on, let's go."

They go out of the house and get into the big white wedding car. The car will take them to the church for the wedding.

"How long will it take to get to the church?" Lydia's father asks the driver.

"About fifteen minutes. There is a football match on in the town, so there are many cars on the road. But don't worry. We will get to the church on time!" says the driver.

The car starts to move. Lydia, her sister and her father are sitting in the back of the car.

Lydia looks out of the window. "My last fifteen minutes of single life!" she says. The car moves slowly. There are many cars on the road. The car stops at a red traffic light. Then, the traffic light changes to green, but the car doesn't move.

Lydia looks at the driver. "The light is green," she says.

The driver looks worried. "There is a problem," he says. "The car won't move."

"What?" says Lydia. "It won't move? Is it broken?"

The driver doesn't answer. The car starts to move slowly. The driver parks the car at the side of the road. The car engine stops.

"I'm sorry," he says. "There is a problem with the car."

"But this is my wedding!" says Lydia. "I have to get to the church! What am I going to do?"

"I'm sorry," says the driver. "I'll call the company and ask them to bring a new car."

The driver calls the wedding car company. He talks to someone. Then, he turns around and looks at Lydia and her family.

"I'm very sorry," he says. "There are no free cars."

"But I have to get to my wedding!" Lydia is nearly crying.

"Don't worry, we will get to the church," says her father. "Come on, let's get out of the car. Maybe we can find a taxi."

"There will be no taxis," says Lydia. "All the people going to the football match will be using the taxis."

They get out of the car.

Lydia starts to cry.

"Don't cry," says Katy. "And don't worry. We will get there."

Just then, a gang of men on motorbikes stops at the traffic lights. The men are big. They have tattoos on their arms. Their bikes are very noisy. They look very bad. They are looking at Lydia and her sister and father. The biker at the front of the gang looks at the other men. He points to Lydia. The lights change to green, and the bikers ride to the side of the road. They stop in front of the wedding car.

"What do they want?" asks Lydia's father.

The biker at the front of the gang gets off his bike and takes off his helmet. He has long hair and tattoos on his face.

"Is there a problem with the car?" he asks.

"Yes," says Lydia's father.

"Where are you going?" asks the biker.

"St Andrews church," says Lydia's father.

"We will take you," says the biker.

Lydia, Katy and their father look at each other.

"How can you take us?" asks Lydia.

"On our bikes!" says the biker. "Come on! There are four of us. You can ride on the back of our bikes."

In the church, Ben is worried. He looks at his watch.

"Lydia is not here yet," he says to his friend Paul.

"Don't worry," says Paul. "There are many cars on the road today."

"But she is thirty minutes late!" says Ben. He looks around the church. Everyone is looking worried. "Maybe she doesn't want to marry me," he says sadly.

Just then, everyone hears a noise outside the church. The noise is very loud. It is the noise of motorbikes.

"What's that? Who's that?" says Ben. He stands up and walks to the back of the church. Paul goes with him. They go outside the church.

"What?" Ben and Paul are very surprised.

They see Lydia, Katy and their father on the back of motorbikes. Lydia gets off the bike and hugs the biker. "Thank you so much!" she says.

Her father and Katy get off the bikes. The bikers wave and then ride down the street.

"Lydia! What is happening?" asks Ben.

"I will tell you later!" says Lydia. "It's a little late, but let's get married!"

3. THE KICKBOXER

Olga has been doing kickboxing for fifteen years. She was the national champion last year. She practices every Monday, Wednesday and Saturday.

Now, she is tired. It is Monday night. She finished kickboxing class thirty minutes ago. She has no food in her house, so she goes to a convenience store to buy some dinner. There are no other customers in the convenience store.

"Hi!" she says to the cashier. She goes to the convenience store very often, so she knows the staff very well. Tonight, Nelly is working. Nelly is a student. She works part-time in the convenience store because she needs money. Olga likes her.

"How is your study?" asks Olga.

"It's OK," says Nelly. "I have a big test next week. I am busy studying for the test."

"You will be fine," says Olga. She goes to the large refrigerator, and picks up a packet of egg sandwiches. She also picks up a protein drink.

What else do I need? she thinks. *Ah, yes, I need some bread for breakfast tomorrow morning.*

She goes to the bread area and looks at the bread. She can't see Nelly, but she can hear her scream.

"Ahhh! Help! Help!" shouts Nelly.

Olga runs to the counter. She sees a man. He is wearing black clothes. He has a black cover over his face. He is holding a long knife.

"Give me the money!" shouts the man.

Nelly is crying. She starts to open the cash register. The man cannot see Olga. She is behind him. She kicks him very hard in the back. The man falls forward and his head hits the counter. He drops the knife. Olga throws her shopping on the floor. She lifts the man up from the counter and pushes him on the floor.

"Quick, Nelly! Call the police!" she says. The man tries to stand up, but Olga pushes him down again. She sits on the man's back.

Nelly calls the police. The man is still moving.

"Nelly! Sit on his legs!" says Olga.

Nelly sits on the man's legs.

Olga takes the black cover off the man's face. He is a young man, maybe 25 years old.

"Why did you do that?" asks Olga.

"I wanted money," says the man. "You are very heavy. Can you stand up?"

"No," says Olga. "You will escape."

Then, they see a police car outside. Two policeman and a policewoman get out of the car and run into the convenience store.

Olga and Nelly stand up. The police take the man away. A policeman stays with Olga and Nelly and asks them questions. They tell the policeman about the man, and about Olga kicking him in the back.

"I was very lucky," says Nelly. "I had a kickboxing champion in the shop with me."

"Yes, you were lucky," says the policeman. "But this is a dangerous job for you. It is late at night, and you are working alone. That is not good."

"It is a dangerous job, but I need the money. I am a student," says Nelly.

"I have an idea," says Olga. "Come to my kickboxing class. I will teach you how to fight."

"That's a good idea!" says Nelly. "I will join your kickboxing class when my big test has finished!"

4. THE NURSE ON THE PLANE

Lucy is excited. She is going to Hawaii with her husband for two weeks. She works in a hospital in New York. Every day, she is very busy. Now it is her summer vacation. She wants to relax on a beach in Hawaii for two weeks. She wants to swim and read books. She doesn't want to think about work.

Now, she is on the plane with her husband Sadiq. She looks out of the window. She can see the sea.

"We will be there soon," she says to Sadiq. "The sea looks beautiful from up here. I'm so happy. Our vacation has started. I don't want to think about the hospital for two weeks."

Just then, there is an announcement on the plane.

---- *Excuse me passengers. Is there a doctor on this flight? If you are a doctor, please tell one of the flight attendants. Thank you.'*----

Lucy looks at Sadiq. "Why do they need a doctor?" she asks.

"Maybe someone is sick," says Sadiq.

They look around the plane. No one calls a flight attendant. No one stands up.

Ten minutes later, they hear the announcement again.

---- *Excuse me passengers. There is a medical emergency. If you are a doctor, please tell one of the flight attendants. Thank you.'*---

Lucy is worried. "There are no doctors on this flight. I am a nurse. Maybe I can help."

"I think you should try to help," says Sadiq.

Lucy calls a flight attendant.

"Excuse me," she says. "I am not a doctor, but I am a nurse. Can I help?"

"Oh, yes please," says the flight attendant. "Please come with me."

Lucy stands up and goes to the back of the plane with the flight attendant. She sees a woman lying on the floor.

"This passenger is having a baby," says the flight attendant. "Can you help?"

"The baby is early," says the woman. "Please help me! It is coming soon!"

"OK," says Lucy. "Don't worry, and don't panic. I will help you."

She looks at the flight attendants. "Please bring me some blankets and gloves. And please bring a pillow for the lady's head."

She looks at the woman. "What's your name?"

"Susan," says the woman.

The flight attendants bring blankets and a pillow.

"OK Susan, is it painful?" Lucy asks the woman.

"Very painful," says Susan. "I...can't...talk..."

"OK, don't talk. Just try to relax. Are you alone?"

"Yes," says Susan. "I went to New York to visit my family. I live in Hawaii with my husband. He is waiting for me there."

Lucy puts blankets under Susan. A few minutes later, she sees the baby's head.

"The baby is coming," she says to Susan. "Please push hard."

Susan screams and pushes very hard. Soon, the baby comes out.

Lucy smiles. "Well done, Susan! It is a girl!"

She wraps the baby in a blanket and give her to Susan. Susan smiles. The flight attendants smile. "Well done!" they say.

Lucy stays with Susan for the rest of the flight.

"Can I announce it to the other passengers?" asks a flight attendant.

"Sure," says Susan.

Sadiq is worried. *Is Lucy OK?* he thinks.

Then, he hears an announcement.

--- *Hello passengers. We have some good news. A passenger had a baby girl. A nurse helped her. The passenger and baby are healthy. The nurse is a hero.'*---

Everyone starts to clap. Sadiq smiles. *Lucy wanted to forget about work and have a relaxing trip. But her vacation hasn't started yet!* he thinks.

5. THE MAN ON THE BEACH

Ethan and Zach are best friends. They are high school students. Now, it is the summer vacation. They are at the beach. It is a beautiful sunny day. There are many other people at the beach. But there is one area of the beach with no people. A homeless man lives on the beach near the rocks. He has a tent. He is old and dirty. People think he is strange. They don't go near his tent on the beach. The man sits outside his tent and watches the people swimming in the sea. He doesn't talk to anyone.

Ethan and Zach are sitting on the beach. They look at the man. He is about 200 metres away from them.

"Why does he live on the beach?" asks Ethan. "How does he get food?"

"I think he goes fishing," says Zach. "And people leave food on the beach. I think he eats that."

"He is strange," says Ethan. "He has been living on this beach for many years."

"Maybe he likes it here," says Zach.

"Maybe," says Ethan. "But no one talks to him, and he doesn't talk to anyone. I'm sure he is lonely."

"Maybe he doesn't like people," says Zach. "Come on, let's go swimming. The water looks wonderful."

Zach and Ethan go into the water. It is very warm. They swim out into the sea. There is a sign in the sea. The sign says, "DANGER! DO NOT GO PAST THIS SIGN!"

"Why is it dangerous?" asks Zach.

"I don't know," says Ethan. "I'm not scared. Let's go past the sign."

"I don't think it is a good idea," says Zach.

Ethan laughs. "You are scared!"

"I'm not scared. But I don't think it is a good idea," says Zach.

"I'm going past the sign," says Ethan.

He swims past the sign. "See? There is no problem," he says. "Come on!"

"No," says Zach. "I'm staying in the safe area."

"Wait…something is pulling me down," says Ethan. He tries to swim back to Zach, but he can't. "The water is very strong here. I can't swim."

"Ethan! Ethan! Are you OK?" shouts Zach.

The water pulls Ethan under. "Zach! Zach! Someone! Help!"

Just then, Zach hears someone swimming towards them. It is the old man. The old man swims past the sign and swims under the water. A few seconds later, he lifts Ethan up. Ethan can't breathe very well. The man holds Ethan and swims back to the safe area.

He swims to some rocks. Ethan, Zach and the man sit on the rocks. Ethan is coughing. He looks at the old man.

"Thank you," he says. "But why did you save me?"

"I saw you go past the sign," says the old man. "I thought, 'The boy is very stupid. It is very dangerous. If I don't help him, he will die.' I have been living on this beach for fifteen years. Sometimes people swim past the sign. I always help them."

"We thought you were a strange old man," says Ethan. "But you are a hero."

Zach smiles. "When we think of heroes, we think of Batman or Superman. But there are many kinds of heroes."

The man smiles. "Go back to the beach," he says. "And don't swim past the sign again!

THANK YOU

Thank you for reading Everyday Heroes. We hope you enjoyed the stories. (Word count: 3,362)

If you would like to read more graded readers, please visit our website http://www.italkyoutalk.com

Other Level 1 graded readers include
A Business Trip to New York
Adventure on the Mountain
A Homestay in Auckland
A Trip to London
Dear Ellen
Emily's Bag
Haruna's Story Part 1
Haruna's Story Part 2
Haruna's Story Part 3
Jimmy Luther
Ken's Story Part 1
Ken's Story Part 2
Life is Surprising!
Ryokan Life
Saori and the Storm
Strange Stories
The Christmas Present
The Old Hospital

Wei's Part Time Job
We Met Online

ABOUT THE AUTHOR

I Talk You Talk Press is an award-winning Japan-based publisher of language textbooks, graded readers and language learning/teaching resources. We won the Language Learner Literature Award in 2019 and 2020.

Our team is made up of highly experienced language teachers and translators, who have all studied at least one additional language to an advanced level.

This experience enables us to design our materials from the perspective of both the teacher and the learner. We consult with both teachers and language learners when designing our textbooks and graded readers, and test our materials extensively in the classroom before publication.

We are a fast-growing press, and currently publish graded readers for learners of English. We publish new graded readers monthly.

Everyday Heroes

Everyday Heroes

www.ingramcontent.com/pod-product-compliance
Lightning Source LLC
LaVergne TN
LVHW051517170726
843492LV00002B/985